Ask Dr K Fisher

about Animals

Written by
Claire Llewellyn

Illustrated by
Kate Sheppard

KINGFISHER

Claire
(the author)

Kate
(the illustrator)

First published by Kingfisher Publications Plc in 2007

10 9 8 7 6 5 4 3 2 1

1TR/0307/TECH/SCHOY/157MA/C

ISBN: 978 07534 1385 2

Copyright © Kingfisher Publications Plc 2007
Text and concept © Claire Llewellyn 2007

Managing editor: Carron Brown
Designers: Joanne Brown, Jack Clucas, Tony Cutting, Amy McSimpson
DTP manager: Nicky Studdart
Senior production controller: Jessamy Oldfield
Cover designer: Jo Connor

Photograph on p10 (top-right): Robert Nunnington/Gallo Images/OSF

A CIP record is available from the British Library.

Printed in China

Kingfisher Publications Plc,

New Penderel House,

283–288 High Holborn,

London WC1V 7HZ

www.kingfisherpub.com

Ask Dr K Fisher about...

Here's a concerned crocodile mum

Snappy with worry

Dear Dr K Fisher,

I'm a Nile crocodile and a responsible parent. My eggs are everything to me: I guard them, help my young to hatch and then protect them from danger. Some reptiles I know desert their young. I can't help worrying about the poor little things. Should I call the police?

Uneasy, in the Nile

4

Dr K Fisher
Any problem solved!
1 Diving-in-the-Water,
Birdsville KF1 1YZ

Dear **Uneasy,**

There really is no need to worry. Most young reptiles - including lizards, snakes, tortoises and turtles - manage without any parental care. The mother just lays the eggs in the ground and leaves them to develop. When the time is right, they hatch by themselves and get on with their lives. It's true, not all of them manage to survive, but many do. You crocodiles make loving mums but I'm afraid you're the exception to the reptile rule.

Kind regards,

Dr K Fisher

tortoise

turtle

lizard

snake

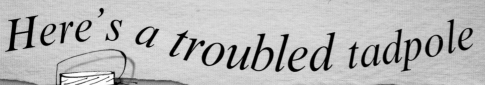

Here's a troubled tadpole

Freaked out!

Dear Dr K Fisher,

I thought I was a tadpole, but now I'm not so sure. My body is changing in alarming ways. My head's bulging, my tail's disappearing and things are beginning to sprout on my body. What is happening to me?

Panic-stricken,
in the pond

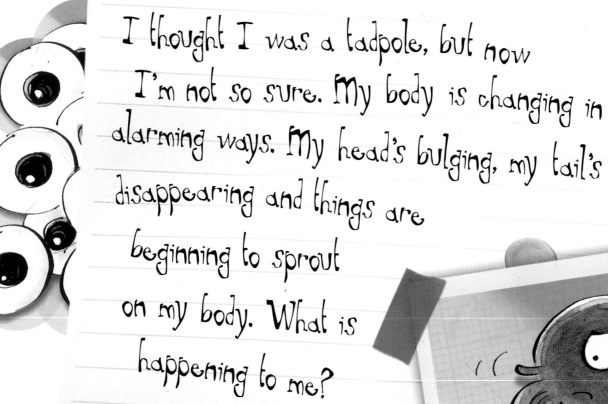

tadpole

6

Dr K Fisher
Any problem solved!
1 Diving-in-the-Water,
Birdsville KF1 1YZ

Dear **Panic-stricken,**

Don't worry – you are perfectly normal. You're just growing up, and that means you're changing into a frog. Most animals just get bigger as they grow, but you change into something completely new. Those sprouting things will soon be legs for jumping. You'll also get lungs to breathe in air. All these changes, from an egg to a frog, are part of your wonderful life cycle.

Good luck!

Dr K Fisher

egg

tadpole

froglet

frog

Turn the page for **more** on **life** cycles...

7

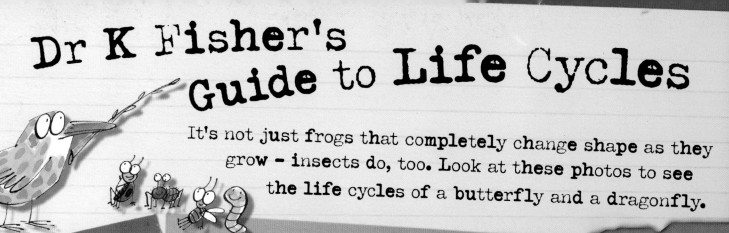

Dr K Fisher's Guide to Life Cycles

It's not just frogs that completely change shape as they grow – insects do, too. Look at these photos to see the life cycles of a butterfly and a dragonfly.

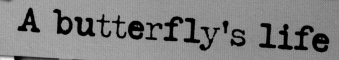

A butterfly's life

My life began as an egg on a leaf.

I hatched into a caterpillar, and ate until my skin split.

My skin moulted four more times. Then I changed and became a pupa.

Then I grew into a beautiful butterfly!

A dragonfly's life

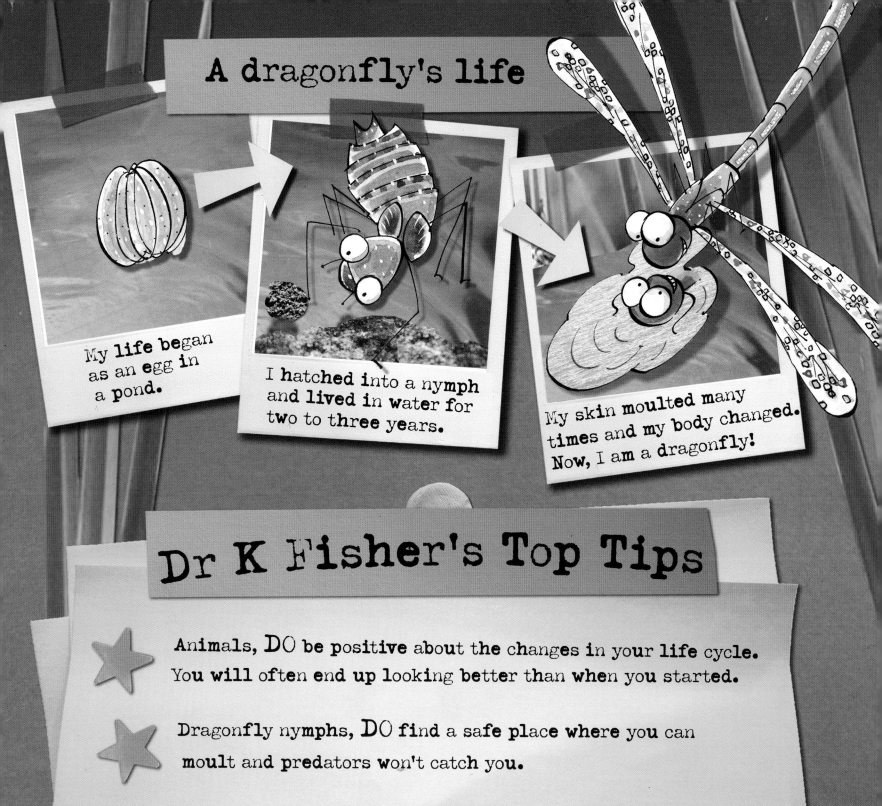

My **life** began as an egg in a **pond**.

I **hatched** into a **nymph** and **lived** in water for **two** to **three years**.

My **skin** **moulted** many times and my body **changed**. Now, I am a **dragonfly!**

Dr K Fisher's Top Tips

Animals, DO be positive about the changes in your **life** cycle. You will often end **up** looking better than **when** you started.

Dragonfly nymphs, DO find a safe **place** where you can **moult** and predators **won't** catch you.

Butterflies, DON'T move inside your **pupa** too much – a **predator** may spot the slightest twitch.

9

Here's a weaverbird with a construction problem

How can I build a better nest?

weaverbird (male)

weaverbird (female)

Dear Dr K Fisher,

I'm a young male weaverbird and I can't build a nest. The grasses come loose, the shape is wrong, the whole thing is a mess. Girls are interested only in boys who can build. Why is a nest so important to them and how can I make one?

Bungling Builder,
in the bush

Dr K Fisher
Any problem solved!
1 Diving-in-the-Water,
Birdsville KF1 1YZ

Dear **Bungling Builder,**

Weaverbird girls get to choose their mate and the one

thing a girl wants is a good, strong nest for her eggs.

Weaving a nest is fiddly work and takes a lot of practice.

From the sound of it, this is your first breeding season

and, to be honest, you stand little chance against the

more experienced males. Try to forget about girls this

year. Focus on your nest-building skills. I'm sure

next year your luck will change.

Best wishes,

Dr K Fisher

adoring females

Here's an embarrassed giraffe

A **tall** story

Dear Dr K Fisher,

I'm a giraffe with long legs and a gangly, 2-metre long neck. I'm so tall, it's embarrassing. All the other animals stare at me, and it's awkward bending down to their level. Why am I so tall, and is there anything I can do to be more like the others?

self-conscious, in the **savannah**

zebra

goat

antelope

giraffe

Dr K Fisher
Any problem solved!
1 Diving-in-the-Water,
Birdsville KF1 1YZ

eats from
top of tree

Dear **Self-conscious,**

You should be thankful for your neck: it helps you get a meal. There's not a lot to eat in your neck of the woods (excuse the pun) – just a few thorny acacia trees. Other animals chew the tough branches at the bottom of the tree. But only you, with your long legs and neck, can reach the tender, leafy branches at the top. You are a very lucky animal indeed!

Kind regards,

Dr K Fisher

eat from
bottom
of tree

Turn the page for **more**
on **feeding...**

Dr K Fisher's Guide to Feeding

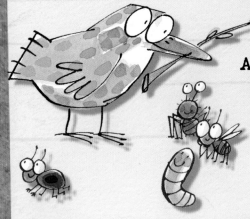

All the animals on this page have developed very long body parts to **help them feed** on their favourite food. It's taken them thousands of years to **develop the perfect body part**.

Elephant

Habitat: Grassland and forest
Diet: Grass, roots, bark and fruit
Special body part: 2m-long trunk for digging and pulling

Aye-Aye

Habitat: Forest
Diet: Nuts, shoots and insects
Special body part: Long finger hooks insects out of bark

Flamingo

Habitat: Lake and lagoon
Diet: Snails, worms and shrimps
Special body part: Long neck reaches down to lake bed

Toucan

Habitat: Rainforest
Diet: Fruit
Special body part: 25cm-long beak reaches fruit at the end of twigs and branches

Anteater

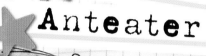

Habitat: Grassland and forest
Diet: Ants and termites
Special body part: 60cm-long sticky tongue mops up insects

Dr K Fisher's Top Tips

★ Finding food is a lot of effort. DO feed on food that others cannot reach. Life will be much easier.

★ If your chosen food is small in size (like ants), or short in goodness (like leaves), DO be prepared to gather a lot.

★ DO make use of any body part you have (tusks, hooves, paws, claws, tentacles or teeth) in order to find your food.

15

Here's a mackerel that wants a change

TIME TO LEAVE?

Dear Dr K Fisher,

I'm a mackerel and I'm fed up with swimming in the shoal. Millions of us mackerels swim together. We're all identical to one another and where the others go I have to follow. Sometimes I crave a different life – one in which I can be myself and do my own thing. Would I be foolish to leave the shoal and strike out on my own?

Want To Be Alone,
in the sea

mackerel

Dr K Fisher
Any problem solved!
1 Diving-in-the-Water,
Birdsville KF1 1YZ

Dear **Want To Be Alone,**

Without question, you are safer in a shoal. The open sea has few places to hide, and a lone mackerel is an easy target for sharks and other hunters. The shoal offers you safety in numbers. If a shark approaches, you all bunch up together. If it charges, you dart off in different directions, leaving the shark confused. Unless you want a short life, I must advise you to stay where you are.

Yours sincerely,

Dr K Fisher

shark

17

Here's a ladybird with a spotty problem

Don't look at me!

Dear Dr K Fisher,

I'm a ladybird and I'm covered in spots. Whatever I do, I can't get rid of them. I try to hide myself away but there's no way anyone can miss me because my wing cases are bright red. Please, please send me a cure!

Feeling Awkward, in the ivy

ladybird

twelve-spotted ladybird

two-spotted ladybird

fourteen-spotted ladybird

Dr K Fisher
Any problem solved!
1 Diving-in-the-Water,
Birdsville KF1 1YZ

water ladybird

pine ladybird

Dear **Feeling Awkward,**

The very idea of a ladybird hiding away! Quite apart from being a handsome beetle, you are colourful and spotted for a reason. Most insects hide to avoid being eaten, but you have a better way to survive: you smell and taste very bad. Any bird that tries eating a ladybird spits it out on the spot, and never makes that same mistake again because your bright colours help to remind it. Far from being a weakness, your looks are your greatest strength!

eyed ladybird

Warm regards,

Dr K Fisher

nine-spotted ladybird

Turn the page for **more** on **warning colours...**

Dr K Fisher's Guide to Warning Colours

Many animals **have** stings and sprays to **defend themselves when they're under attack. These animals have bright colours** or markings, **which advertise their powerful weapons and warn predators to keep away!**

WARNING

poison-arrow frog

Brightly coloured skin contains a deadly poison

WARNING

skunk

Bold black-and-white stripes warn others of its evil-smelling spray

WARNING

coral snake

Red, yellow and black rings advertise its poisonous bite

WARNING

bee

Yellow-and-black stripes tell the world that it has a painful sting

Dr K Fisher's Top Tips

 If you **have warning** colours, DO make sure **everyone** can see them. It's no good **hiding yourself** away.

 DO **have confidence** in your warning colours, **even if you are** unarmed. Hoverflies flaunt their stripes and they can't sting.

 If a **predator** gets too close in spite of your warning colours, DO hiss, **buzz** or **puff yourself up** to scare it away.

21

Here's a lovesick spider in deadly danger

Date or dinner?

Dear Dr K Fisher,

I'm a male orb-web spider and I need your help. There's a sweet spider around here and I'd really like to get to know her better. But I've heard some terrible rumours: do girls really kill boys after mating? Though I'm keen on her, I'd like to survive. What do you think I should do?

Lovesick But Wary,
on the Web

orb-web spider (male)

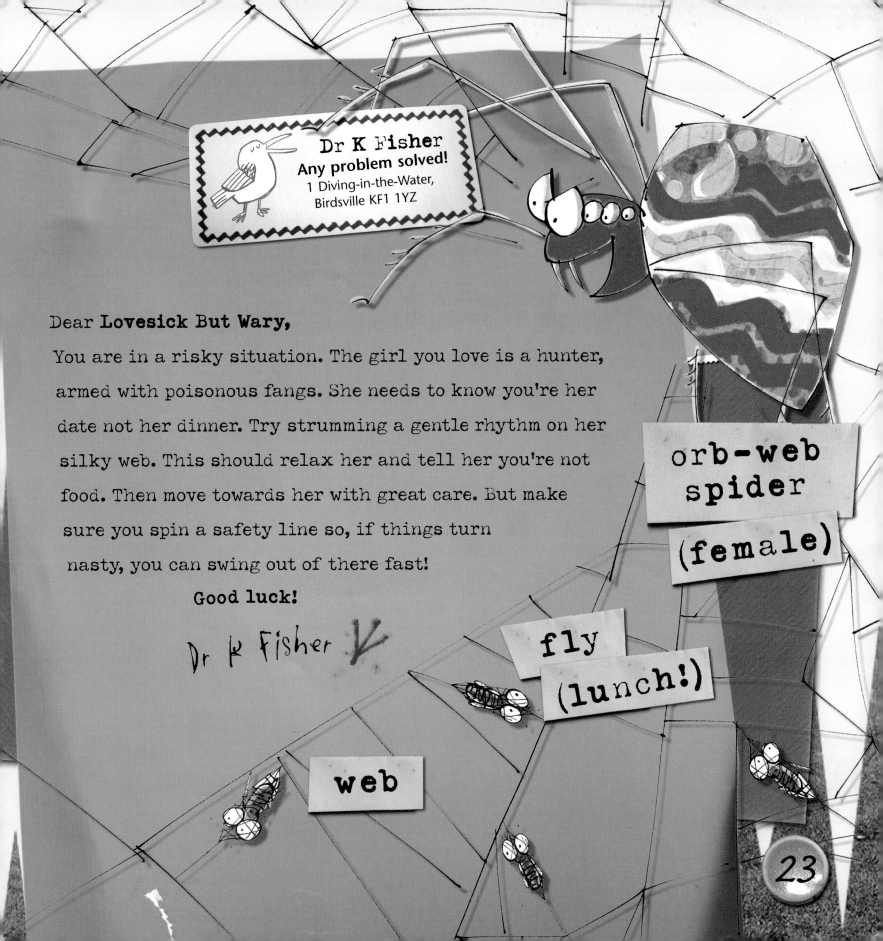

Dear **Lovesick But Wary,**

You are in a risky situation. The girl you love is a hunter, armed with poisonous fangs. She needs to know you're her date not her dinner. Try strumming a gentle rhythm on her silky web. This should relax her and tell her you're not food. Then move towards her with great care. But make sure you spin a safety line so, if things turn nasty, you can swing out of there fast!

Good luck!

Dr K Fisher

orb-web spider (female)

fly (lunch!)

web

23

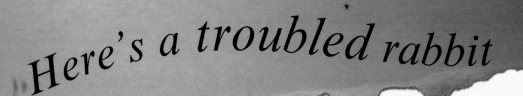

weasel

Grass is best

THE MEADOW
2ND SEPT
POST

Dr. K. Fisher

Dear Dr K Fisher,
I'm a rabbit and I would
like to know why so many
animals want to eat me.
I'm hunted by weasels,
owls, foxes, cats, dogs,
stoats and ferrets. Why
can't everyone just eat grass
and try to get along?

Give Peace A Chance,
in the meadow

rabbit

24

Dr K Fisher
Any problem solved!
1 Diving-in-the-Water,
Birdsville KF1 1YZ

Dear **Give Peace A Chance**,

The world is not perfect for rabbits, but nor is it perfect for foxes and owls. These meat-eaters (known as carnivores) have to catch every meal. They eat plant-eaters (known as herbivores) who, in turn, eat plants. Carnivores, herbivores and plants – you're all connected in a food chain. I would advise you to count your blessings. Your long ears help you to hear trouble coming, and you can run very fast.

All good wishes,

Dr K Fisher

fox

Turn the page for **more** on **food chains...**

25

Dr K Fisher's Guide to Food Chains

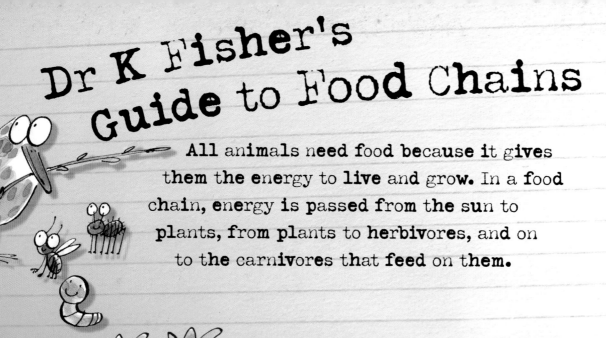

All animals need food because it gives them the energy to **live** and grow. In a food chain, energy is passed from the sun to plants, from plants to **herbivores**, and on to the carnivores that **feed** on them.

An Arctic food chain

I EAT

I EAT

moss (plant)

caribou (herbivore)

wolf (carnivore)

A rainforest food chain

I EAT ↓

I EAT ↓

fruit (plant)

monkey (herbivore)

eagle (carnivore)

Dr K Fisher's Top Tips

 Carnivores, catching food is never easy. DO try to avoid injury and keep yourself in tip-top condition.

 Herbivores, DON'T worry too much about being prey. Many of you have big families and always outnumber the hunters.

Everyone, DO look after plants. They supply us with food to eat and without them we would starve.

27

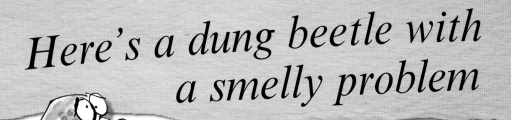

Life stinks!

Dear Dr K Fisher,

I'm a young dung beetle and I've made a shattering

discovery: all I can eat is dung (poo)! The other dung

beetles are obsessed with it, and race off to gobble up

droppings as they splat on the ground. Or they roll

it into balls, take it home and lay their eggs in it.

Yuk! Why do I have this disgusting diet?

Outraged, among

the cowpats

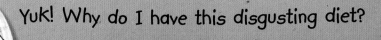

dung

beetle

28

Dr K Fisher
Any problem solved!
1 Diving-in-the-Water,
Birdsville KF1 1YZ

Dear **Outraged,**

I sympathise, I really do, but many creatures have a taste for dung. Along with flies, worms and bacteria, you are one of nature's rubbish recyclers, and you do the world a great service. Without you, we would be drowning in dung. By eating it and breaking it down, you recycle the important nutrients it contains – and make the soil a better place, where plants can live and grow. Be proud of the work that you do!

Yours respectfully,

Dr K Fisher

flies

worm

29

Glossary

 bacteria
Tiny creatures that live in soil, water and air.

 hatch
To break out of an egg.

 carnivores
Meat-eating animals.

herbivores
Plant-eating animals.

develop
To grow and change.

life cycle
The growing process of an animal or a plant, from the start of its life until it is fully grown.

 diet
The food an animal naturally eats.

moult
To shed skin during growth so that the body can grow bigger.

 habitat
The natural home of an animal or plant.

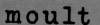

30

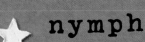

nutrients

Substances that can be taken in by an animal or plant to help it grow.

nymph

The young life stage of an insect, which later changes into an adult without becoming a pupa.

predators

Animals that hunt other animals for food.

prey

Animals that are hunted and eaten by other animals.

pupa

The stage in an insect's life when it changes into an adult.

recycle

To break down something into simple parts, which can then be used again.

reptiles

Cold-blooded animals, such as snakes, that have tough, scaly skin and live on land.

savannah

Dry grasslands in east Africa.

Index